The Chinese Man and the Chinese Woman

by John Lewis · illustrated by Peter Rigby

Bergström + Boyle · London / Two Continents · New York

A few words before we start the story

This book isn't meant to be like a Chinese dictionary. The story is a way of showing how the Chinese picture words of long ago can still be seen in Chinese words today.

A picture of a couple of trees for example—means "forest."

This is the second book in a series that began with "The Chinese word for Horse" which had the title word on the cover.

Here are some other characters from the first book...

RAIN CLOUD.   SWORD.   GROWING FIELD.   CART.

The simplest word for man is little more than two legs.
The tall man with feet firmly on the ground and
head above the sky is a gentleman and
a knight.

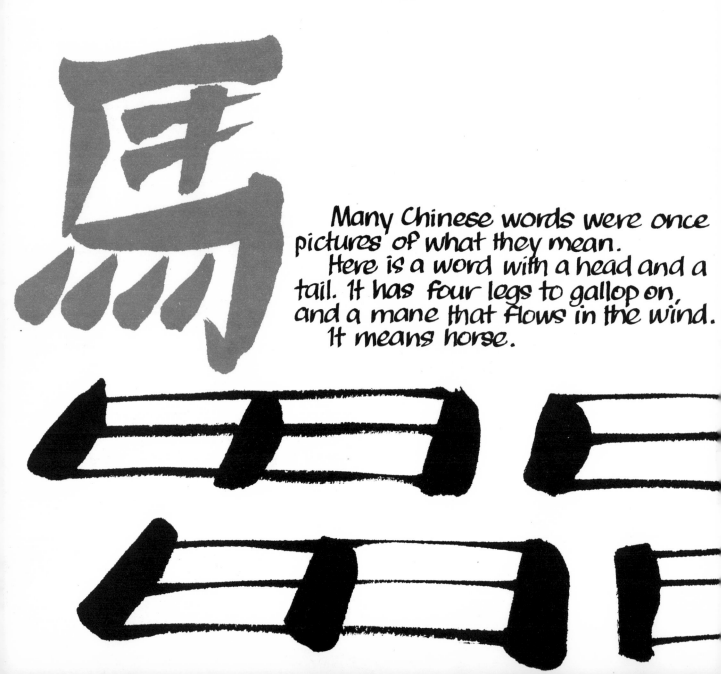

Many Chinese words were once pictures of what they mean.
   Here is a word with a head and a tail. It has four legs to gallop on, and a mane that flows in the wind.
   It means horse.

This particular horse used to have
a fairly good time simply galloping
around and around in the fields.
A square divided into four is the
Chinese for fields. Fields with sprouts
are growing fields.

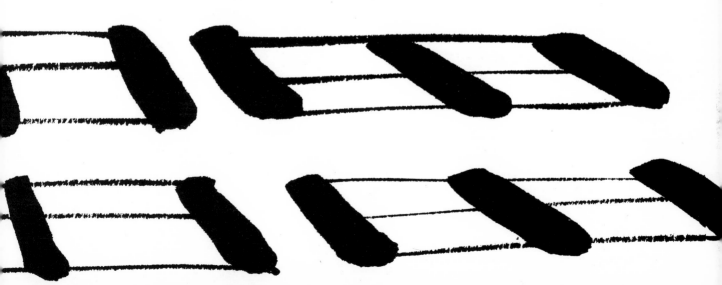

馬夫刀

The fields stretched almost to
the eastern horizon where you can
see the sun rise on clear blue days.
        The fields and the horse belonged
to a farmer who wore in his hair
the Chinese pin that marks a man's
coming of age.

        Although the horse had a fairly
good time galloping around by himself,
he enjoyed it much more with the man
on his back swishing his sword.

The man would swish his sword on the one side and then on the other, shouting: "Haw!" or "Yaw!" or "Yawhaw!"
They did this day after day till they got tired of it.

The man said to the horse, "It may be amusing to a horse to go galloping around and around day after day, but it's not much of a life for a man of property."

The horse didn't say a word.

This man became very unhappy.
"Look at all my fields," he said.
The horse looked at his fields.
"Look at my horse."

The horse looked over his shoulder
at himself and swished his tail.
"Look how proudly I stand and
carry my sword.
I have all this, and yet I need
something more."

Just to be friendly, the horse said,
" You have a cart as well.

"What good is an old creaking cart?" the man complained. "Do I have so little to be proud of, that I have to be proud of a cart? A cart is for a simple farmer, not for a gentleman. I need something else."

"You have a shed," the horse added quietly.

"A shed!" the man shouted. "A shed is just a roof to put over a cart." And that is what the Chinese word for shed looks like.

The man sat himself down on a stool
and gazed into the trees beyond his fields.
    The morning song of birds seemed to
give a voice to every branch. You can see
three open mouths of birds in the trees
in the Chinese word for birdsong.
    How can you listen to birds singing and
not be happy?
    "Why am I unhappy?" he asked.

是 馬

Around him flowers were opening
to the sun. How can you sit among flowers
and not be happy?

"Why am I unhappy?" he asked again.

The horse said, "If you want to know why
you are unhappy, you will have to go and
find a man who is happy, and ask him
what makes him happy."

The farmer sighed and climbed on the
horse saying. "I should have known that
a horse couldn't have the right answer.

The Chinese word for gate looks like a gate.
They rode out through the gate into the world.

They found a man who had only a few
fields, and yet the man was happy. Beside
him was the woman that you can see in this
Chinese word. The man's wife was helping
him in the fields. They were both happy.

"Good morning," the horseman said,
"What makes you such a happy man?"
The man said, "I don't know. When you are
happy you never ask yourself why."

They rode on. Now and then the knight
swished his sword, but he got no pleasure
out of it. He said, "Haw! Yaw!" and "Yaw! Haw!"
several times, but his heart wasn't in it.

They came to a second man resting in the shade of a tree. He had a happy smile on his face.

"Why the happy smile?" asked the rider.
"I'm simply happy," the man said, "I've no idea why, but my wife is happy, too, perhaps she can tell you."
They turned and asked the wife.

She said modestly, "My husband can answer any question better than I can. Whatever I want to know, I ask him."

So they rode on. Clouds cut out the warmth of the sun. A cold, heavy rain began to fall. The man was more unhappy than ever.

He said, "Haw!" and began to take out his sword. Then he put it back again. They sheltered under some trees.

The horse saw how unhappy his master was and he made a suggestion, "Each of these men had a wife - perhaps they are happy because they have wives to keep them company."

The man pooh-poohed the idea,
"If company were all 1 needed, 1
would be happy because 1 have a horse.
Let's ride on - the rain is letting up."

They met a third man. He, too, had
a wife. He was a happy man, as well.

"Can you tell me," asked the horseman
again, "What makes you happy?"

"1 cannot tell you," said the man,
"I'm only a poor farmer. 1 have no horse,
1'm not a swordsman. Your sword would
look clumsy in my hands - 1 suppose
1 am just easily contented."

The rider was thoughtful as they rode on.
Then he said to the horse, "It may be that,
because you are only a horse and cannot
be as wise as a man, you looked for a
simple answer and found the truth.

Now I, being wiser, was looking for
an answer that needed a lot of thinking
about."

The horse listened carefully,

The man continued, "There may be
something in the answer you have stumbled
on: all these men had wives and all these
men were happy."

The horse said, "Look, there's a young
woman in that field. She doesn't appear to
have a husband."

"I can see what you're thinking," the
man said, "if I ask the young woman to
be my wife then I, too, will be happy? Is
that so? Again, I must remind you that
a man is wiser than a horse. Look at that
young woman - have you ever seen
anyone so unhappy. All the men we met
had happy wives. We must ride on."

Further on they heard singing. It was beautiful singing. They followed the sound of the singing until they came upon another young woman happily working by herself.

The man smiled knowingly at the horse, "You see, he said, that is the kind of woman to make a man happy."

The man went without delay and asked the young woman to marry him.

"Marry you?" she said, "I've already promised myself to another man."

He put his head between his hands.
"The only woman I can find who doesn't
seem to be married is an unhappy woman."

"I was unhappy yesterday," the woman
said, "but then a man asked me to marry him."

The horse looked at the man. The man
looked at the horse. Then he leapt onto
the horse and rode off swishing his sword,
shouting, "Haw!"

They returned at full gallop till
they came near where the unhappy
woman worked in the fields alone.
When they could see her the man
reined in his horse and walked
quietly over to the woman.

夫 女

The man stood in front of the
woman. She looked up. He said,
"I have come to ask you to be my wife."

The young woman looked at
him in surprise. Then she looked
down at the ground. The man had
to kneel to see her face.
   And when he looked at her face,
he saw that she was smiling.

He carried her away on the horse
to his many fields and they were married
and lived happily.

The horse riding swordsman took great
pride in being a husband. He was still
proud to swish his sword. He was proud of
his horse and his fields. He was even
proud of his old cart shed.
And he was happy.

And that is why the Chinese word for
contentment is a roof with a woman
under it.

Man

Woman

Contentment

Sunrise

Gate

Stool

Flower

Shed

Birdsong

First published by Bergstrom + Boyle Books Ltd
22 Maddox Street · London WIR 9PG · 1977

Published in the United States by Two Continents
Publishing Group Ltd · 30 East 42 Street · New York · NY/10017

Made and printed in England by
Burlington Press · Foxton · Cambridgeshire

Production services by
Book Production Consultants,
7 Brooklands Avenue · Cambridge

Bergström + Boyle   ISBN 0 903767 11 2

Two Continents   ISBN 0 8467 0384 X